Reflections

Reflections
  Women's Struggle for Justice and Equity

©2024 Renwick Rose

Published by Hobo Jungle Press
St. Vincent & the Grenadines, W.I.
Sharon, Connecticut, USA

ISBN #979-8-9897406-3-5
Library of Congress Control Number: 2024942259
First edition
November 2024

This is the first in a series entitled *Reflections*
Other titles in the series include:
We Grandparents' Back Pay – A Struggle for Reparatory Justice
Reclaiming Our Independence and Defending Democracy

All rights reserved. No part of this publication may be reproduced, distributed, or transmitted in any form or by any means, including photocopying, recording, or other electronic or mechanical methods, without the prior written permission of the publisher, except in the case of brief quotations embodied in critical reviews and certain other noncommercial uses permitted by copyright law.

Reflections
Women's Struggles for Justice and Equity

by Renwick Rose

Acknowledgements

While I am the author of the articles published in this booklet and the others in the series, it stands to reason that these could not be the product of an individual, certainly not of my own making. While I have been engaged in writing for more than half a century, and it has crossed my mind that I should attempt at least a compilation of my written material, circumstances and perhaps insufficient personal commitment in this direction have dictated otherwise.

Over the years I have been approached by several persons inquiring when I am going to publish. While I do appreciate their concerns, most of them genuine, I am acutely aware that there are some more interested in what I would have to say that could strengthen their political pursuits or just being malicious. It must be remembered that I have not only been actively involved in social and political struggles over the 50+ years but that I have been on the ground here all that time.

Last year I was approached by a group of patriots about working together to get my written materials published in a book. Given the credentials of the group and my own unfulfilled plans in this direction, I consented and began drawing up an outline for this publication. We began the process of compilation and embarked on the process.

So, first I must acknowledge the massive contribution of my support team and particularly, at the core, Sis. Clare Keizer with whom I forged an invaluable working relationship while she was editor of the SEARCHLIGHT newspaper of which I am a director, but more so, a weekly contributor since its inception in 1995.

Also contributing, in addition to his role as a member of the organizing team, is another long-standing colleague, Brother Fadhilika Atiba-Weza. Atiba, despite his half a century in the diaspora, has always kept in touch with the progressive nationalist movement at home. He was a leading member of the overseas brigade of the United Peoples Movement (UPM) and has contributed positively to enhancing the progressive focus of many in the leadership of the Vincentian diaspora. His involvement in this project is another manifestation of this.

My heartfelt thanks also to those patriots who have provided insightful introductions to the various booklets in the series. Sis. Nelcia Robinson has already made her mark in the regional and international women's movements and in civil society as well. Incidentally, I have known her since secondary schooling beginning in 1959, and we were colleagues in the leadership of the now defunct UPM and in the regional civil society movement as well. My gratitude to her knows no bounds.

In the same light, I am deeply honoured to have the distinguished regional jurist, Justice Adrian Saunders, consent to do the Introduction to the section on "Kill the Bills" in the booklet on *Reclaiming Our Independence and Defending Democracy*. Justice Saunders was a leading figure in that 1981 mass movement as well as its legal advisor. He was also a close colleague of mine in the UPM, following in the footsteps of his late brother Ronnie, in the active demonstration of his patriotism. His consent to give his blessing to our work is but another manifestation of his commitment to democracy.

Dr. Garrey Dennie is an outstanding Vincentian historian, currently one of four scholars appointed to document the first authentic history of St. Vincent and the Grenadines. He is also a strong advocate for reparatory justice for the victims of slavery of African people, genocide of indigenous people and colonial plunder in the Caribbean. I am humbled to have him contribute to our effort on "Reparations", another publication in the series.

On the artistic side, the booklets on "Women" and "Kill the Bills" both are enhanced with graphic illustrations. It is instructive that when I approached a longtime Brother and Comrade of mine, Glenroy "Sulle" Caesar about contributing his considerable artistic skills to our efforts, he did not hesitate in replying within minutes in the affirmative. Sulle is a two-time calypso monarch of St. Vincent and the Grenadines, a leader in social commentary, among them songs on reparations and "We Need a Rescue Mission" (in the aftermath of the U.S. invasion of Grenada) four decades ago. He is also an outstanding artist, poet and drummer. That is not all, for Sulle's political credentials are embossed in the work of YULIMO and the UPM, the successful battle to "Kill the Bills" and for national independence. My abounding gratitude!

Having written this series, I think it appropriate to acknowledge the role of some of the leaders of that epic battle against the 1981 bills who have since departed this world. SVG owes a lot to: Comrades Caspar London of the UPM and the National Progressive Workers Union (NPWU); Oscar Allen of the UPM; former Parliamentarians Sister Yvonne Francis-Gibson, Calder Williams and Parnel R. Campbell; Sister Earlene Horne of the National Farmers Union; Brothers John "Damani" Williams and Glenroy "Santana" Gordon, both of Questelles and the UPM; farmer Stafford Bute of the NFU; trade unionists Cyril Roberts, Jerry Harewood, Wilberforce Emmanuel, and Sister Alice Mandeville of the CTAWU.

Many others still alive deserve our eternal respect.

Much appreciated!

– Renwick Rose

Contents

Introduction	ix
Preface	xiii
WOMEN'S STRUGGLES	1
Women and Politics	3
Women and the Struggle for Equal Rights	5
Women's Demands Linked to Democratic Demands	8
Sexual Imagery Damaging Young	10
Women Press For Progress: The Time Is Now	13
Women Can Uplift the Whole Society	16
Women Are Not Baby Factories	18
WOMEN'S ADVANCES	21
Honouring Women in Business, Trade Unionism	23
Women in Kaiso	26
Females Playing Leading Carnival Roles	29
Women and Technological Development	30
Women's Advances in World Sport - Football	32
SECTORAL ISSUES	35
Mother's Day Under Covid-19	37
The Nurse – An Extraordinary Human Being	40
Abuse of Female Domestic Workers Must Be Ended	42
INTERNATIONAL WOMEN'S DAY	45
IWD and Women	47
IWD and the Progressive Movement	49
International Advances for Women, But SVG Still Lagging	51
Women's Day Must Bring Us Together	54
IWD – Rooting Out Violence Against Our Women	57
IWD 2022 – Much to Celebrate	60
IWD 2021 – Women, Let's Choose to Challenge Ourselves	62
Making Gender Equality a Reality	64
GENERAL	67
Just A Kiss? / Oh Africa!	68
Thank You, Mama.	71
About the Author	73

Introduction

by Nelcia Robinson-Hazell

Nelcia Robinson-Hazell is a Garifuna poet, community organizer and activist from St Vincent and the Grenadines. She has, for several decades, spearheaded the development of policy initiatives throughout the Caribbean on issues regarding gender and indigenous identity.

The role of women in sustainable development in the history of our country has been continuously overlooked by many historians. Oral tradition has brought their stories to the forefront. However, there is a tendency to dismiss these stories as myths and fables, and to relegate women's roles to housework and dutiful lovers. Nevertheless, much information on the role of women remains untold, because writers of early history did not see the importance of the role of women.

This publication should, therefore, serve as an incentive and encouragement to current researchers to continue their deep dive, because many questions remain unanswered.

Early history and oral tradition of European encounter and conquest of the Indigenous People of Hairoun/Yurumein, now known as St. Vincent and the Grenadines, tell of Baruda, wife of Paramount Chief Joseph Chatoyer, who chided him for frequently wearing women's clothing, as he often wore hers when he was defending the island against the colonisers. Chatoyer told her that his attire formed part of his strategy to move among the colonisers undetected, and to allow him and his warriors to gather information for planning purposes, and also to execute their defense.

Joseph Chatoyer, our National Hero, was neither afraid nor ashamed to call upon the strength of women in the fight for freedom. He, however, chose to be 'invisible' as a man, and the enemy appeared not to know him, because the legend has it that Major Leith, his opponent, once asked him: "Are you Chatoyer?"

It can, therefore, be said that woman's "invisible" image allowed Chatoyer to walk freely among the enemy, to gather information and to plan strategies that allowed our country to have a greater measure of freedom from colonial domination.

Likewise, the advocacy of Comrade Renwick "Kamara" Rose challenges the invisibility of women, and acknowledges the wealth of resources for the nation's development when they are clothed with recognition and dignity.

In these Chapters, Kamara fearlessly bares his thoughts. He has no need to be "invisible", as he acknowledges women's contribution as an important pillar on which society stands. He also challenges women and policymakers to do more and to fulfil the various Declarations and Plans of Action designed for the advancement of women.

As Editor of the FREEDOM Newspaper, organ of Youlou United Liberation Movement (YULIMO), Kamara gave a strong voice to the then Women's Movement.

The first celebration of International Women's Day took place in 1974, and this was the forerunner to the United Nations endorsement in 1977.

There were four international conferences which followed this landmark annual activity.

In 1975, the Commission on the Status of Women called for the organization of the first world conference on women to coincide with International Women's Year. It was held under the theme Equality, Development and Peace.

The 1974 Article, which was titled Women and Politics, lamented women's inequality as it highlighted issues and supported women's cry to "stand up and make a choice for themselves", and asked the question: "Are we going to live this meaningless life, deprived of the power of control over our lives, exploited, "sexploited" and dehumanized?"

In highlighting women and the struggle for Equal Rights, a 1978 article boldly stated, "Here in our country the status of women is truly a disgrace. Women are still discriminated against, left, right and centre. This discrimination is backed by bourgeois values which serve to encourage male domination and the continued subjection of women."

As if in response to such advocacy, the 1980 World Conference had as its theme, Employment, Health and Education. A Programme of Action called for stronger national measures to ensure women's ownership and control of property, as well as improvements in protecting women's rights to inheritance, child custody and nationality.

In 1985, the World Conference to Review and Appraise the Achievements of the UN Decade for Women took place in Nairobi, Kenya. The mandate of this conference was to establish concrete measures to overcome obstacles to achieving the decade's goals. Governments adopted the Nairobi Forward-Looking Strategies for the Advancement of Women, which outlined measures for achieving gender equality at the national level and for promoting women's participation in peace and development efforts.

In 1987, the JUSTICE newspaper, with Renwick Kamara Rose as editor, exposed deficiencies in the system. Issues such as equal pay for equal work, paid maternity leave, equal opportunities and benefits for children born to unmarried women, were among 10 critical areas of concern for the advancement of women. This was eight years ahead of the 12 critical areas of concern in the Beijing Platform for Action 1995.

The burden of violence against women was addressed during the International Women's Day activities in March 1988. In his deeper analysis of the underlying causes and factors which give rise to acts of violence committed against women, Kamara said that: "...in holding up the banners of justice and equality for women, we need to recognize that the inequality that women face is part and parcel of the inequality which characterizes itself in our society itself...the struggle against the oppression of women is inextricably bound up with the struggle against all forms of oppression.."

The 1995 Fourth World Conference on Women marked a significant turning point for the global agenda for gender equality. The Beijing Declaration and the Platform for Action is an agenda for women's empowerment, and is considered the key global document on gender equality. It outlines 12 critical areas of concern for the advancement of women. These include Women and Poverty; Education and Training of Women; Women and Health; Violence against Women; Women and Armed Conflict; Women and the Economy; Women in Power and Decisionmaking; Institutional Mechanisms for the Advancement of Women; Human Rights of Women; Women and the Media; Women and the Environment; and the Girl Child.

While the United Nations (UN) carried out five-year reviews to assess progress, Kamara was doing a critical analysis of Government and NGO performance towards the achievement of the established goals. It would seem that the Beijing Platform for Action had accomplished its goals, and advocates were now resting on their laurels.

Kamara was persuaded that it was time to lengthen the stride, not to slow it down. His writings in the SEARCHLIGHT newspaper on the occasion of Women's Day 2010 noted that there were international advances for women, but SVG STILL LAGGING! I, therefore, encourage you to read the book to get his analysis of why there are so few women in Parliament.

Moreover, articles written by Kamara and published in 2017, 2018, 2020, and 2023 take the reader into the areas of sport, culture and activism, as he calls upon women to challenge ourselves to bring about positive change.

Kamara writes with heart and compassion. He is jealous in his thinking that the dark side of the oppression of women must not prevail, and zealous in playing his part of intervention and prevention. I encourage you to consider his beautiful tribute to our Mothers, including their challenges under COVID-19, and his compassion for female domestic workers who suffer abuse. I also encourage you to read and to be enlightened and motivated, in a bid to also play your part in the journey towards the advancement of women.

As the 30-year review of the Beijing Platform for Action approaches, this booklet, therefore, emerges as a reminder of the struggle and the achievements, and it will also serve as a guide for advocacy, as well as a warning to "Touch Not the Women."

Preface

I first started writing for public consumption in 1972, the year I first got involved with progressive politics, becoming a foundation member of what we grandly called the Black Liberation Action Committee (BLAC). This organization, in addition to its local aims, announced lofty global ambitions ("the liberation of black people everywhere") as well.

With no training, no experience in journalism, I took on the responsibility as editor of, first, our occasional leaflets which were distributed freely, and by August of the same year, our fortnightly newspaper, FREEDOM, published in stencilled form but with a printed cover page, and sold to the public for the princely sum of 25 cents. The responsibility fell in my lap principally because I was then teaching at a secondary school and most of the members of our organization had a limited educational background.

I must credit my mother for equipping me for this challenge, not just from the parental duties of educational opportunities, but also because of her love of reading and writing. She was, right up to her later stages, a regular contributor to the local press. It would be remiss of me, too, not to give credit to two women who have rendered priceless support, encouragement and assistance for much of my writing career. I refer to my wife, Ancelma and to Sister Erica Morgan-Nichols, who worked alongside me in my various endeavours.

It is now more than a half a century since I have been writing in the local press, with the responsibility of editing as well as chief correspondent for almost 20 years. I have also been serving as a weekly columnist and member of the Board of Directors of one of our country's major newspapers, SEARCHLIGHT.

As a weekly columnist, I have touched on a wide variety of topics, local, regional and international in scope and covering political, cultural, sporting, and social issues. Among these, I found myself drawn to issues affecting the rights of women and the need to address the inequalities and discrimination that continue to oppress them to this day. Again, I credit my mother for this, for she was a strong advocate of women's (and children's) rights.

It was therefore no surprise that the very first issue of FREEDOM had a full-page article, penned by me, but with the input of the few sisters then involved, entitled, "Women and Politics", calling for women to take a more active role in politics and in fighting for their rights. This began a long commitment in the press as well as in activism to women's issues.

This book reproduces some of the articles on the subject that I have written over the years, some published as editorials in the papers with which I have been associated. I do hope that they would give readers a better understanding of how many of the issues facing women were addressed in my humble writings and contribute, not only to a greater appreciation of women's struggles, but to inspire you, women and men alike, to play your part in this noble struggle for justice for women and children.

My thanks to the support group that has helped to initiate this effort and to make this, and subsequent publications, a reality. Eternal Gratitude!

– Renwick Rose, 2024

Reflections on Women's Struggles for Justice and Equity

WOMEN'S STRUGGLES

Women and Politics

For years now, the system has ignored the Black woman and kept her completely out of political life. Currently faced with the emerging new Black Woman, a politically conscious woman, there is an attempt to influence and control the direction of the Black movement by bringing our women under their control...

If we examine the present situation, we will realize that Black women are completely cut off from politics, whether conventional or unconventional. The conventional politics, or politricks as YULIMO calls it, is dominated by a few. In addition, politics is completely dominated by men. Though black men have little power over decision-making, they feel justified in at least discussing politics.

The Black woman on the other hand, does not feel that she even has this right. To her, politics is the concern of her man. Save for a few exceptions, notably the Labour Party's Women's League and the PPP stalwarts, the typical response of the Black woman is, "I'm not interested, politics is not for me". As for those involved with the politrickal parties, they, like poor lost sheep, are being misled by the politrickans and have a completely false idea of politics with the result that they end up misusing their energies and skills for wrong purposes.

The answer to this lies not, as the system tries to convince us, in placing a few more women in governmental positions- female Ministers, female Governors etc., but to bring about a revolutionary change in the whole system of politics whereby both black men and women would have full participation in the decision-making process.

We should remember that politics is the process which directs our day-to-day lives. As such then, all black people should have the right to decide how our lives should be run. In other words, politics is the responsibility of each and every one of us and not just a few politrickans. When we consider the position of the Black woman in society, the wife and mother, we realize that in her daily life she encounters politics at every turn. The food she eats, the prices she pays for that food, the values she gives her children, the school to which she sends them, the kind of education her children get, the clothes she wears, her form of entertainment, all these are influenced by political decisions.

It is this situation that we must seek to correct in order to bring an end to the evils of this corrupt colonial system. We have to stand up and make a choice for ourselves. Are we going to live this meaningless life, deprived of the power of control over our lives, exploited, "sexploited" and dehumanized? Does the solution lie in trying to get a visa and run off to North America and England and becoming a second-class citizen there?

We, the women of YULIMO, say "No". We must stand up as proud Black women and accept the fact that we have a RIGHT to make decisions about the way that black people must live. In other words, politics is her business, She has the right to determine the destiny of her people. Sisters, we must get ourselves fully involved in the struggle for our rights. We must ORGANIZE to end our oppression.

– FREEDOM *newspaper, August 1, 1974*

Women and the Struggle for Equal Rights

On March 8, working women all over the world will celebrate International Women's Day. The commemoration of this historic and important day immediately brings to mind the status of women in our society. In local upper- and middle-class circles, talk on the topic is heard every now and then, but the status of women has remained the same.

It has been correctly pointed out that in any society, the level of women's development gives a good indication of the overall level of development of that society. Here in our country, the status of women is truly a disgrace. Women are still discriminated against left, right and centre. This discrimination is backed by bourgeois values which serve to encourage male domination and the continued subjection of women.

In St. Vincent and the Grenadines, women are conditioned from their earliest years to prepare themselves for the role that society has carved out for them: baby-makers, housekeepers, maids and in general as domestic conveniences for men. The lack of adequate day-care centres, kindergartens and equal employment opportunities, force many of our women to spend their lives tied to the home, completely dependent on their men. Where women are offered jobs, they are paid less than men for the same work and their prospects for promotion are certainly not as high as their male fellow-workers.

Under these conditions it is no wonder that they are unable to fully reveal their talents and potential.

The result is that society regards women as inferior and fit only for their traditional roles. As long ago as the 1860s, one writer noted that Nature has given women a trusty, strong and penetrating mind. But society does not benefit from this mind because "it rejects it, crushes it, and stifles it. The history of mankind would advance ten times faster if that mind were not rejected and killed but was active."

In these circumstances it is downright nonsense and a mockery of women to pose the question, "are women ready for equal rights?" as one local newspaper did some time ago. Instead of asking such a foolish question, we should really ask, how can women achieve equal rights? Under which type of society is it possible for women to achieve equal rights?

Under the system of capitalism, there can never be genuine equality between the sexes. Where the means of production of a country, that is the factories, banks, large estates, big businesses etc., are owned by capitalists, inequality of the sexes is used as a tool for the making of greater profits and the only source of their concern is how to make greater profits. This is why the liberation of women cannot be separated from the struggle of the working class against capitalism. Unless the women's movement grasps this vital and significant fact, it will make little or no progress. Instead, the movement will be led astray by the bourgeois notion that "men" constitute the problem. In fact, right now, the problem is capitalism and what is the answer? The struggle for socialism.

In the African countries which had to wage an armed struggle to achieve their independence, the women's liberation movement was speeded up due to the fact that many women fought gun-in-hand alongside their male counterparts. They showed just as much courage, determination and strength as men. They proved that women are not second-class citizens.

In the countries that have already achieved socialism, women are guaranteed all the rights afforded men, not only by law, but more importantly, in actual practice. The socialist countries are noted for the high degree of women's involvement in all fields of activity. In the Soviet Union, International Women's Day has been declared a public holiday in recognition of the outstanding role women have played in the development of that country.

Here in Youlou (SVG), the women's movement is still weak and ineffective. A strong, dynamic, democratic women's organization is lacking; an organization with a working class outlook that is prepared to link the struggles of women against discrimination with the struggles of all the exploited and oppressed peoples against imperialism; an organization which will put endless pressure on the government and ruling class to ban male chauvinist advertisements, end prostitution by providing work for the sisters, and open up avenues for women to take their rightful place alongside men.

As another International Women's Day comes and goes, YULIMO, as the vanguard of the working class, pledges its total solidarity with the women of Youlou (SVG), the Caribbean and the entire world. As has always been the case, we will continue to give our support to these struggles and to uphold the rights of women and all other exploited and oppressed strata.

– FREEDOM *newspaper, editorial, March 3, 1978*

Women's Demands Linked to Democratic Demands

International Women's Day activities this year focus on violence against women in an attempt to sensitize the society and galvanize action to eradicate this cancer from our midst.

There is a general tendency to sit up and take notice of violent assault on women only when it has reached outrageous proportions as in recent cases of the brutal rape and murder of young girls. More subtle, but nonetheless degrading acts of violence against women tend to be taken for granted.

Because of this, responses to such acts are most often sporadic and focus almost instinctively on calls for stiffer penalties for sex offenders even to the point of such mediaeval forms of punishment as flogging.

True, the law must prescribe fitting penalties for those who violate the dignity of our women, but we must not deceive ourselves into believing that such legal steps and implementation of such punishment are by themselves a cure-all for violence against young girls and women.

There is a need to go much deeper to probe the underlying causes and the factors which give rise to acts of violence being committed against women. In so doing, in holding up the banners of justice and equality for women, we need to recognize that the inequality that women face is part and parcel of the inequality which characterizes itself in our society itself.

To be sure, there are features peculiar to women, but in a general sense every disadvantaged group in our society faces discrimination. It is in this sense that JUSTICE always contends that the struggle against the oppression of women is inextricably bound up with the struggle against all forms of oppression.

For this reason, those of us who believe in justice, fair play and equal opportunity cannot afford to be mere bystanders as the women's movement makes its demands. We need to give active support and help to relate and link those demands to the broader demands of the oppressed and underprivileged sections of our society.

In turn, the women's movement must avoid the error of seeing itself in very narrow and limited terms; in raising its voice only when the interests of women are affected in a very direct sense. If it is to gain that credibility, that level of acceptance and support by the broad mass of people, men and women alike, it must also be prepared to speak and act in defence of broad democratic rights as well.

Violence against women does not occur in a vacuum hence one must be able to relate it to such issues as those portrayed in the media; the level of education in the society; unemployment and the like. Such an approach places challenges before us all – the women's movement, its friends and supporters alike.

In this light it is pleasing to note the continuing emphasis being placed by sections of the women's movement on the need for proper support services for women. Unless we can lift the most oppressed and desolate of our women out of the quagmire of poverty, ignorance and misery, we are never, ever, going to be able to accomplish such lofty goals as eradicating violence against women.

– JUSTICE *editorial, March 11, 1988*

Sexual Imagery Damaging Young

On Wednesday of this week, the women of WINFA organised a live radio call-in-programme to highlight issues concerning violence against women. Part of the focus of this programme was directed at violence perpetrated against young women and how this violence is linked to wider societal problems. It is for the Caribbean a critical social issue, in St. Vincent and the Grenadines especially. Shockingly, a United Nations Report documents our country as having the THIRD HIGHEST RATE OF SEXUAL OFFENCES per head of population IN THE ENTIRE WORLD. (SVG, Poverty Assessment Report 2008).

The manifestations are with us weekly – reports of child molestation; sexual abuse of young girls; and while there does not appear to be widespread organised prostitution, there is sufficient evidence to suggest that in an informal sense, many women, young and not so young, are selling their bodies, and images of themselves, for material gain. Worse, in the media today, women's bodies are being used as "hard sell", for products (particularly alcohol) and for promoting entertainment activities. The saddest aspect of this is that it is the young, the teens and even pre-teens, who are the chief targets. Recently there was even a despicable ad on local television involving the use of school uniforms in far from wholesome activities.

We are not alone in this mess; it has become a global curse with many nations struggling to combat it, not always with a great deal of success. In Britain for instance, a recently-published Report is occupying the attention of law-makers in Parliament. This Report, the result of research work done for the British Home Office by a leading psychologist, Dr. Linda Papadoupolos, concludes that children are being over exposed to sexual imagery and that parents are increasingly powerless to stop it.

The Report makes a clear link between sexual imagery and violence towards females. It cites materials such as the increasingly popular 'lads mags' (magazines popular with young males); pornography on mobile phones; and even big-name fashion brands which use sexual imagery to advertise clothes among teenagers. Termed the 'drip-drop' exposure, the psychologist claims that such exposure is distorting the self-perception of young people, encouraging the 'macho' culture of male dominance, while young girls in turn are being encouraged to present themselves as sexually available and permissive.

Do these conclusions ring a bell? Do we not observe similar tendencies here? Daily, the complaints are made. Yet, as a society, as law-makers, educators, parents, community leaders, we seem unable to stem the tide. In schools in particular, the number of incidents keeps mounting up, whilst the public sexually-explicit behaviour of many young people demonstrates a basic disregard for decency and self-respect. One especially negative development is related to the technology of today: the use of mobile phones and social networks to circulate nude or topless photos of women, and even sexual acts.

Dr. Papadoupolos has this to say of this widespread sexualisation: "Unless sexualisation is accepted as harmful, we will miss an important opportunity… to broaden people's beliefs about where their values lie."

These negative trends have their roots in what is happening in the wider society; the promiscuousness, the willful sexual exploitation of women and young girls, the open flaunting of women's bodies and sexual images. Nothing is taboo any more. The youngest child sees more of these images in one week than a person of 25 years would have seen in a whole year some three decades ago. The changes in the society mirror these realities.

Since I was using a UK reference, let me go there to show how those changes facilitate the sexualisation process. Another Report there reveals how social life is changing dramatically. This Report shows a sharp decline in the number of post offices, libraries and traditional pubs. You know what are replacing them? Gambling houses, casinos, clubs and gentlemen clubs, with lap-dancing and striptease acts! Since 1997, the number of police stations in the UK has decreased by 160, hospitals clinics by 580, schools by 2,380 and libraries by 200. By contrast, whereas there were only 24 lap-dancing clubs in 1997 there are now over 300. What message is the youth getting?

That is the social milieu of today's world, a world where in spite of the many achievements in helping to bring about gender equity, our young women and girls are rapidly being parachuted down the other side into a world where their bodies are considered as mere commodities to be used, abused or cast aside at the whim and fancy of their abusers. This then is the big challenge before our women, as we move into International Women's Day on Monday, March 8th.

– SEARCHLIGHT *newspaper, March 5, 2010*

Women Press For Progress: The Time Is Now

I extend warmest greetings to my Sisters of all ages and on all continents, on the occasion of International Women's Day, which was celebrated yesterday, March 8, 2018, under the theme – THE TIME IS NOW!

Vincentian women, following in the tradition which began here in 1975, engaged in different activities to mark the occasion, though on a personal level, I would have liked to see a more coordinated and robust response. Significantly, it was the non-governmental sector, the progressive movement in particular, which led the way in placing the commemoration of IWD firmly on the local calendar, and I am eternally proud to have made some little contribution to the effort.

Today, there are visible signs of women's progress in our society, as women become more assertive and occupy positions of influence, in the public sector in particular, but also increasingly in the professions, and to a lesser extent, in business as well. Female presence at leadership level can be evidenced in the Teachers' Union, continuing the tradition of again electing female leadership under the presidency of Sister Wendy Bynoe, to whom I extend congratulations and best wishes.

There is also a significant female presence in the media, even reaching right to the top, in ownership (Ms. Desiree Richards at the VINCENTIAN), and management (Ms. Clare Keizer, managing director of Interactive Media Ltd, publishers of SEARCHLIGHT, who wrote an excellent editorial in the Midweek edition earlier this week).

Yet, while we must celebrate these advances, it must not blind us to the fact that we still have a long way to go to overcome the legacy of centuries of discrimination against women, in our society and globally. The Secretary General of the United Nations, in an address to mark IWD 2018, put the matter squarely before us all as follows:

"Achieving gender equality and empowering women and girls is the unfinished business of our time, and the greatest human rights challenge in our world."

In the address, the UN leader explained that there are still "serious obstacles" in the way of addressing what he called "the historic imbalances that underpin discrimination and exploitation". It is a charge reinforced by the Secretary General of CARICOM, pointing to a global pay gap, which results in women earning 23 per cent less than men, and in the fact that women constitute less than 20 per cent of landholdings worldwide. This continuing inequality is so glaring that the World Economic Forum noted this year that, "2017 was the first time in more than 10 years that the gender gap began to widen again."

In SVG, quite rightly, there has been much emphasis on a particular aspect of the injustice against women: that of violence against women, including sexual assaults, even of minors. This is laudable, but it must also be placed in the context of the wider social and economic injustices against women in our society; and our women, whatever their partisan political views, must never allow the Women's Movement to lose sight of the broader objectives.

We still have a long way to go towards the consolidation of a solid national women's movement, diversified in its many aspects, but united by common goals. There ought to be greater clamour and demands for stronger recognition of the fight for women's rights and social justice for them. The attitude of both political parties over the years, while laudable in strengthening legislation, has been lacking teeth in strengthening and adequately resourcing departments which are charged with the responsibility of supporting the struggle to end discrimination and exploitation of women. It would be good if our women leaders, for a start, would begin to address this matter.

To quote again from the UN statement, "We are at a pivotal moment for women's rights". It is simply unacceptable to excuse any forms of violence against women, whether sexually, domestically, economically or socially.

THE TIME IS NOW! Let us all PRESS FOR PROGRESS!

– SEARCHLIGHT *editorial, March 10, 2018*

Women Can Uplift the Whole Society

I offer my salute to the women of this nation as they prepare to celebrate yet another International Women's Day (IWD) next Monday. We in St Vincent and the Grenadines have been observing this most international of global activities since the year 1974, being one of the first in the Caribbean to do so consistently.

Over those years, IWD has met our women facing all sorts of challenges, but in terms of impact, perhaps none as deep-seated as this one in the wake of the COVID-19 pandemic. Not only have there been dangers to health and life, but the disruption in the economic and social life of our people has been severe. Working mothers have been particularly hard hit with lay-offs, especially in the hospitality industry, and reduced incomes or in many cases none at all save for state assistance.

There is also the social problem of the enforced closure of schools, even pre-schools and day-care centres, leaving mothers with the additional problem of trying to take care of their children while seeking alternative employment or sources of income.

While it is true that fathers have, in the last decade or two, become more supportive and cooperative in handling such domestic problems, there is still a high degree of irresponsibility on the part of men in our society. Those who claim almost a divine right to leadership must understand that it carries with it the weight of responsibility. It is no wonder that the themes for this year's IWD revolve around issues of challenging and leadership.

International Women's Day is not about platitudes congratulating women and then back to square one on March 9. It is true that the position of women in our society has improved over the years. Women are now prominent in leadership positions in many areas of public life. But the real test of the progress of women is that such advances on a personal or organisational level must begin to generate an upliftment for the status of all women. The society itself can only benefit if those at the bottom are uplifted, for they will raise the entire society with them.

Those who are privileged to earn leadership positions must themselves become advocates for those at the bottom of society, be the voices for the voiceless. They must use their positions of influence to shed light on the continued discrimination against women as a whole, to draw attention to the plight of women and girls in deprived communities, rural and urban. Women who occupy important positions must use the levers at their disposal to trigger mechanisms for firm action to end the scourge of violence against women. We cannot be satisfied with just marches and rallies on November 25 each year, we NEED ACTION NOW!

Disrespect and disregard of the rights of any woman must become an affront to all women. The campaigns against the sexual exploitation and harassment of women must be given the full, public and enthusiastic support of women in influential positions and organisations with considerable influence. We must begin to challenge those responsible for the dispensation of justice for the relative leniency sometimes shown towards sexual offenders and perpetrators of violence against women. And, "women of substance" must begin to demonstrate their mettle by treating their domestic workers with respect and dignity, ensuring that they too can lead decent lives for themselves and their families. We will all be better off because of it.

These are some of the challenges before our women, and by extension us all as we mark IWD next week. The challenge for an end to inequality and injustice, crimes which affect women in particular, begins with us on a personal level and goes right up the society. We have much to celebrate on IWD 2021, but we must acknowledge that we have a long way to go and commit ourselves to staying the course.

– SEARCHLIGHT *newspaper, March 6, 2021*

Women Are Not Baby Factories

Our Prime Minister (PM) does not only have his hands full in trying to keep the ship of state on course, but since, like the rest of us he has only one brain, it must run the risk of being over flooded with ideas. His is a herculean task (some of his own making), trying to cope with the multitudinous challenges locally as well as fulfilling the many and ever-increasing international responsibilities.

It is very easy in such circumstances to make unfortunate statements even when well-meaning, so it is important to be very careful in public comments and to get appropriate advice in delicate situations. The PM himself is famous to preface statements by saying "I am advised". So, many people, yours truly included, must have been surprised by the statement reported in

SEARCHLIGHT (31/05/24) and attributed to Dr. Gonsalves which urges women of child-bearing age (25-35 years) to have more children because of our falling birth-rate:

"We need them (women) to have more babies", he is reported as saying. To his credit, the Prime Minister provided a rationale for his appeal, that being the falling birth rate. "We have to replenish the population which is stagnant and growing older". While making it clear that he is not encouraging teenage pregnancy, (indeed his appeal is to working age women), and perhaps following in the footsteps of a predecessor whose advice was to "bat but don't score", he departs from the non-scoring advice, needing the female batters to score.

"The civilization has to find a way of replenishing itself and advancing", he says. "It can't be replenished by people from Mars; it has to be replenished by real flesh and blood women". While it is commendable for the PM to raise such a serious demographical issue which has social and economic implications, it is unfortunate that it is put in a context as though we are discussing low manufacturing or agricultural production.

We are long past the stage when if there is a population problem, we simply call on women to either reduce the numbers of children or, as in this case, to step up "production". Women are not baby factories, they are "real flesh and blood people" as the Prime Minister would remind us. The situation is far more complex than that and an appreciation must be shown for women's productive rights as well as their domestic, occupational and social ambitions.

As the PM himself must be aware, there are several complex societal issues involved and it will take flesh and blood consideration on the part of all involved to find solutions. Having more children is not the only solution to a stagnating population so the discussion must be a holistic one. Whatever the solution arrived at, it can only be taken by the free choice of women, and we must all respect their choices.

We need to go beyond the old sexist approaches. If a baby boom is considered desirable, while it takes two to tango, it is women who bear the brunt of the burden of childbearing and child-rearing. Even where there is support from the other partner, it is women who carry the brunt of the burden. It is they who are often required to forgo personal and occupational opportunities, their time which is most sacrificed.

In recognition of these realities, the first step in handling the looming population challenge is for an open discussion of it, with emphasis on the participation of women. What are the choices before us? To what extent is migration contributing to the current situation and how can this be addressed?

Then there are the distinctly women's issues pertaining to their reproductive and social rights. We must give the "flesh and blood women" a lead in this. Indeed, it would be good to hear frank views of the women in the Cabinet and administration on such issues, unencumbered by party affiliation or loyalty. Or is it that we are about to see a baby boom in those quarters?

At the end of it, for women to acquiesce to the decision to have more babies, it requires incentives by government to women of child-bearing age which address the challenges they must face. In so doing the society has to meet the many sacrifices involved. Each child decision has enormous social, economic and personal implications. We cannot just say that the population is falling, and women must make up the shortfall. We are long past that stage. So, we can start the debate on a more respectful level. What sacrifices by working women will be necessary? How is the broader society, including husbands and partners, to participate both in the discussion as well as in making the sacrifices necessary? What incentives would be appropriate if such a route is chosen?

It is important for women and their organizations of all types to take up the issues involved.

We must ALWAYS RESPECT OUR WOMEN AND THEIR CHOICES.

– SEARCHLIGHT *newspaper, June 7, 2024*

WOMEN'S ADVANCES

Honouring Women in Business, Trade Unionism

One of the effects of the technological and communication revolution has been to spread cultural influences rapidly.

Today's world, its young people in particular, are influenced by practices, thoughts and trends from all over the world. Naturally, those ideas and practices which arise within the countries which have greatest control of the media, or from countries with which we interact most often, exert the biggest influences on our lives, for better or for worse.

Those influences are reflected in almost all areas of human endeavour. We notice them in fashion, food, lifestyles in general. Curiously, we in the Caribbean seem more inclined to adopt or copy practices and trends in many not-too-healthy areas, being more reluctant to embrace more positive features from abroad. In fact, there are some in our midst who are all too ready, under the guise of resisting foreign influences, to condemn any cultural import, no matter how positive.

Take the Black History Month concept for instance. That idea, of celebrating the contribution of black people to human development, took root in North America and is now officially commemorated there in the month of February, (in October in the United Kingdom). Given the ethnic composition of the Caribbean, our common experience of slavery, and our physical proximity to the

United States, it was quite natural that the idea caught on in the Caribbean as well. Yet, there are those among us who openly criticize this commemoration, dubbing it a "copycat" practice. Fortunately, this backward trend has been resisted.

Right on the heels of Black History Month, female rights activists in the USA have been able to win presidential and congressional support for the commemoration of a Women's History Month during the month of March each year. This idea, like the Black History Month, has its roots in the early struggles of women for equality, manifested in the fight to have International Women's Day globally recognized on March 8 each year. It, too, focuses on highlighting achievements and critical roles, this time those of women. This year, the theme for Women's History Month is "Honouring Trailblazing Women in Labour and Business". Is this not a worthwhile initiative? After all, we now stage all kinds of celebrations alien to us, including Valentine's Day and Halloween! Honouring women who have been pioneers in the field of business is certainly a needed venture.

A couple years ago, the Chamber of Commerce and National Properties initiated a campaign to honour Vincentian pioneers in the field of business. Among these, most deservingly, is Ms Erica McIntosh, who has made a name for herself and contributed significantly in the agro-processing field. Many others have gone unsung and it would be good if women like the late Sylvia DaSilva (hospitality industry), Clara Layne (commerce) and Marjorie Tucker (agriculture) were so honoured. There are many others still making contributions today, whose example we must uphold.

In the same light, there are those who have contributed in the field of labour, in trade unionism to be exact. In this field, we have not been kind to the pioneers, male or female. George McIntosh and Ebenezer Joshua overcame this bias to be now in the frontline of those considered for the status of national hero. But Joshua did not accomplish what he did, neither in trade unionism or politics, on his own. At his side was his wife, Ivy Joshua. Was there any woman so denigrated, despite her efforts on behalf of the working class and the indigenous people of North Windward? The old Labour Party did a "hatchet job" on her, spewing ridicule and displaying class, race and colonial bias in the process. It is high time to correct this historical crime.

Many other female pioneers in the field of trade unionism have never been appropriately honoured, or rewarded for their contributions. Among these are one of Joshua's lieutenants, the late Alma Johnson of Old Montrose; a Joshua stalwart who ran the offices of his union and political party. In more recent times was another deceased, Alice Mandeville of the Commercial Technical and Allied Workers Union, as well as another, forgotten, but still alive and active, Cynthia Matthews of the same union. There are others too: Yvonne Francis and Joye Browne of the Teachers' Union, towers of strength in the embattled days of that union's struggle for recognition. What can be wrong in using the Women's History Month idea to focus on the contributions of these heroines?

— SEARCHLIGHT *newspaper, March 3, 2017*

Women in Kaiso

Let me begin by offering my heartiest congratulations to the respective winners of the various Carnival competitions, to the CDC and private entertainment promoters, and above all to the people of St. Vincent and the Grenadines on the successful staging of our historic 40th anniversary of the June/July Carnival. Permit me to also make the point that, in stressing that Carnival celebrations here pre-date 1977, it is important to document the historical record of the original festival and to also celebrate landmarks in that regard.

My very special congratulations too, go out to Lornette 'Fyah Empress' Nedd for her victory in the Calypso Monarch competition, and as well to her sister finalists, one of whom, Joanna Christopher, better known as a national netballer, not only made it to the finals on her first attempt, but finished in third place. This could be seen as the final consolidation of the trend of women coming to the forefront in this once male-dominated field and making their mark at that.

There were many aspects of the Calypso Monarch show, and Carnival 2017 on the whole, which deserve commendation, but forgive me if my focus is especially on our female singers. More and more they are coming to the fore, at all levels, competing with the males and demonstrating their credentials to be treated as equals. In 2017, we not only witnessed an increase in numbers on the 'Big Stage', but also in the quality of their delivery, in what was itself a competition of exceptional quality.

What I found most pleasing, and auguring well for the future, is the fact that, by and large, the female calypsonians of today, have rejected the old role of the degenerating 'wine and grind' calypsonian, the old sexist stereotype. They have brought a refreshing breadth of scope to the topics covered, with assertiveness and social awareness reflected in their choice of topics and the lyrics and forceful presentation offered. In so doing, they have struck a significant blow for women's equality.

There are those among us who are not so comfortable with this new assertiveness; who are uneasy when Shena Collis stresses "No More", a signal that the old days of female inferiority are over. There are those who are unhappy with 'Fyah Empress's strident "Guilty as charged", and even question whether a song with explicit violent content should have emerged victorious. But the calypso judges do not have a mandate to make moral judgements on the songs offered.

In addition, Fyah's message was not so much homophobic, as it was the expressed anger of a wife, who found that she had been deceived by a husband who was in a same-sex relationship. One can frown on her solution, but the very act of bringing the issue to the fore, on such a stage, has to be commended. We have to face up to uncomfortable issues.

In praising the female bards, we cannot ignore the contributions of their male counterparts. They contributed to a competition of a very high standard, propelling the female challengers to greater heights if they were to achieve success. The result was a competition full of pointed social commentary, as contrasted with the mere recitation of facts or allegations. There was also satire and humour, giving a blend of rich quality, deserving of the occasion.

Lovers of the art form can be mightily pleased by what was offered in 2017, in both fields of calypso and soca. For our soca artistes too have been revealing the wealth of talent and creativity which exists among the younger generation. A great future lies ahead if we learn how to harness, develop and sustain this talent which must now be channelled into the year-round entertainment field, creating employment for artistes and scope for the development of the entertainment industry and by extension, the tourism and hospitality industries.

One negative aspect which continues to plague our Carnival, and those in the rest of the region too, is the growing immorality being demonstrated publicly and its impact on our children. It is an issue which must be addressed by us all. The degeneration in moral standards is reaching epidemic proportions and is casting a negative image over the whole of our Carnival. Moral standards must be as much a part of the festival as standards in all other areas.

– SEARCHLIGHT *newspaper, July 14, 2017*

Females Playing Leading Carnival Roles

There has been much positive comment in the media (both formal and social) in Trinidad and Tobago about the increasingly positive role being played by women in Carnival festivities in that country.

Women have always been involved in the Carnival action but it is very noticeable in recent years that their prominence has increased and that more and more men are no longer dominating in certain fields, including leadership. Women are no longer just doing the behind-the-scenes donkey work with the men, who, though equally hard-working, take all the credit.

Whether it is in bandleading, calypso, soca or chutney, women are going "punto-punto" with their male counterparts, and getting the credit for it, though there are still remnants of the old discrimination against them. In the calypso monarch competition, women are more than holding their own and soca divas like Patrice Roberts and Destra Garcia go toe to toe with their male counterparts.

But it is in the steelband movement that progress is especially marked. All the steelbands from schools right up to the mega bands have a significant female presence. Even more encouraging is that the women are not just "playing pan", increasingly there are now female arrangers of even top bands indicating the value of females pursuing musical studies at university level. To crown it off, the umbrella body of steelbands in T&T, Pan Trinbago, is headed by Tobagonian Beverley Ramsey-Moore, and the band which she leads, Katzenjammers, won the national competition for medium-sized bands. Yes, progress to report and of which to be proud.

– February 27, 2023

Women and Technological Development

The month of March, which in the context of its historical significance to St Vincent and the Grenadines ranks alongside August and October, begins tomorrow, March 1. In its designation as National Heroes Month, March occupies a special place and our editions in that month will no doubt reflect that special position, but March also has a broader international significance for us.

For more than a century now, activities have been held all over the world in observation of what is now celebrated globally as International Women's Day (IWD) on March 8. It is a day of tremendous social, economic and political significance since it focuses on the lives of half of the world's peoples, women, and their struggles for gender equality in a still lop-sided world.

Given their role as mothers and lynchpins in the family structure, the focus on women is clearly most relevant and each year themes are developed by the United Nations to highlight particular areas of emphasis on the continuing uphill battle for equality. Significantly, in recognition of the critical role of technology in the modern world, the theme chosen for 2023 is, "DIGITALL: Innovation and technology for gender equality".

It is a most appropriate choice since it places emphasis on the equal part women must play in modern technological development. Historically, although women have continued to demonstrate that they are equally equipped to pursue technological development, their role has always been relegated by the bias of HIS-tory. This is changing, though not fast enough, especially in underdeveloped countries, and today more and more, women are coming to the fore in areas which would have been considered taboo, including such areas as computer programming, space exploration and nuclear physics.

Facing historical discrimination, we must not shy away from what is universally recognized as the need to redress centuries of neglect of the equal role which women should play. Importantly, while undertaking bold initiatives in this regard, we must not wait until women reach community college or university. The outreach must target our females right from the beginning, challenging the traditional roles which had been mapped out for them.

This is critical not only to realizing the goal of gender equality, but in releasing so much potential trapped under centuries of bias and discrimination. It also enables the flowering of our talents and abilities from which the entire society and our national development thrust can only benefit.

Yes, we must continue to fight against the repressive and regressive actions against women; violence, sex trafficking and the like, but we must also place equal emphasis on equipping our women for the world of technology, and embrace and utilize to the fullest, every opportunity for technological development.

– SEARCHLIGHT *newspaper, February 28, 2023*

Women's Advances in World Sport Football

Some of the most promising developments in recent weeks in a world of increasingly gloomy news, have been the clear signs of the steady advances in the position of women in the global sporting arena.

Currently, pride of place is football's Women's World Cup taking place in Australia and New Zealand. This represents the continued expansion of the women's game, for it will be the first time that the World Cup for women is being held in the southern hemisphere and being shared among two nations, Australia and New Zealand. It will be the first time that such countries like Jamaica, Haiti, Vietnam, the Philippines, Morocco and Zambia are represented.

This has its origins in the development of women's sport generally, and in football in particular. While the first World Cup for men was staged in 1930, it took more than 60 years before its counterpart, for females, could be held in China in 1991. Then, there were 12 finalists as against the 32 participating now, including the countries mentioned above.

Football, like many other sports, has suffered from the grave discrimination against female participation in sport. For years, female participation in what was long regarded as a "men's sport", was frowned upon and even banned in some countries up until the 1970s. Even when women were "allowed" to participate, they faced many hurdles and discriminatory practices in terms of levels of support, facilities provided, a lack of appreciation of the need for special assistance and promotion and, you would have guessed it, far unequal payments for participation.

It took very militant action by female footballers in some countries, notably the USA, for equal pay to be recognized, though that is still far from the case in many countries. In a bid to encourage more female participation, the governing body of the sport, FIFA, has guaranteed individual payouts of no less than US$ 30,000 to each participating player with up to US$ 270,000 for finalists. Some FIFA member nations are not happy with the direct payments, but FIFA has justified its actions by saying that it wishes to guarantee that the players themselves get the full sum.

The World Cup, estimated to be watched on television by hundreds of millions worldwide, will certainly provide a platform for a further take off of women's football. But it has a very long way to go in many countries, including our own. We have a long way to go to get young women in schools, particularly at the primary and secondary levels, involved in the sport by providing opportunities and incentives. Yes, it is important to continue to participate in FIFA and CONCACAF tournaments, but we will only be on the move in women's football when we pay attention to the base and remove and dismantle the barriers to female participation.

– SEARCHLIGHT *newspaper, July 25, 2023*

SECTORAL ISSUES

Mother's Day Under Covid-19

I had another Mother's Day, always a very special occasion for me, without my dearly beloved deceased mother, but, I tell you what, I am far from being the only one. Millions of others, here and all over the world, were in the same situation, and lest we feel collectively sorry for ourselves, COVID -19 reminds us that there were others losing their precious mothers on that same Mothers' Day. Just think of our compatriots in New York or the UK for instance, in the epicentres of the epidemic and what some of them must have gone through last Sunday!

Yet, much as we mourn the loss of the bereaved mothers, it is important that we keep focus and think of those, mothers and children alike, having to face the day-to-day effects of the pandemic. Think of the mothers, laid off from their jobs and without incomes, save for the subsidies from the state or state agencies. To make matters worse, some of these have lost the remittances sent home from relatives abroad because they too have become economic victims of the COVID.

In our context, it is important to recognize that many of those directly affected negatively, laid off or with significantly reduced work times, and incomes, are mothers themselves. The workforce in the hospitality industry – hotels, restaurants, entertainment spots – is dominated by women, most of them mothers. "Happy Mothers' Day" must have had a very hollow ring to many of these. That is why, in whatever relief or assistance measures taken, whether by government or private employers, a gender perspective is so necessary. Often, it is not just a female worker sent home; she may be a mother of two or three children, and even the "minder" of an ailing mother at home, the family breadwinner. It is not just her personal welfare on the line, it is the welfare of an entire family.

Then there is the no-small matter of the children and education. Besides the everyday concerns of coping with children in a restricted environment, with no schoolteachers to share the daytime caring burden, the spectre of the new school year, whenever it begins, looms ahead. This is very challenging in normal times, much more so to the resumption after the COVID hit. Even the state will be significantly limited in its means to assist.

In the current circumstances, the emphasis on health and safety is not only understandable, but it is correct. However, one cannot ignore the essential ingredients of food and nutrition. In this respect, I commend the Ministry of Agriculture, spearheaded by Minister Saboto Caesar, for its initiative to provide some nutritional support to needy families in the form of food boxes. The action is all the more commendable in that it is based on local produce, purchased from farmers, thus providing a market for farmers already facing the challenge of exports to "locked-down" or financially affected regional markets.

It is a fact of life, and an irony too, that agriculture and fisheries have turned out to be the sectors of greatest economic opportunity in, not just the current crisis, but in the post-COVID world as well. I reflect on the arguments of the so-called "experts" and short-sighted politicians during the eighties and nineties, virtually tolling the bell on these sectors. Everything pointed to tourism, yes tourism, and information technology as the areas on which we should concentrate. We failed to understand that grasping new opportunities does not mean neglecting the fundamentals. Food is Numero Uno among these. However the world changes, whatever we do, the role of food is constant and agriculture and fisheries will ALWAYS be fundamental.

Avoid Political Connotations

Having said all of this, it is important not to confuse worthy and needed interventions with any sort of political connotations. It is unfortunate that our country and some of its neighbours have to grapple with the pandemic with one eye on impending elections. Whether so or not, every action on the part of those governments, is going to be viewed not on its own merit, but as to whether it is aimed at winning electoral support. Naturally, governments themselves will not be immune to temptation.

Thus, in my opinion, it is a pity that, given the "love" themes used by the ruling ULP in previous initiatives, the "Love Box" should be the name chosen for the laudable nutritional box programme. Inevitably, a most deserving programme runs the risk of being associated with a party slogan. It does not have to be like that.

Naturally, the organisers of this deserving initiative will disagree and point to the absolute NEED for such a programme and its intrinsic value. I agree wholeheartedly, but could we not have avoided the connotation? It is true that every action taken to help alleviate the challenges posed by the crisis will be taken by some as electioneering, but where we can, we must cut the ground from under those who can only see partisanship before them.

The COVID pandemic should be one to bind us together, not one for political bickering over every initiative and criticisms and objections without constructive proposals. Those who behave opportunistically in the crisis will be exposed. It happened before in 1979 in the aftermath of the volcanic eruption. The health, safety and livelihood of our people, not their ballots, must remain foremost in our considerations.

– SEARCHLIGHT *newspaper, May 15, 2020*

The Nurse – An Extraordinary Human Being

By fate or coincidence International Nurses Day (May 12) this year came right amid the heroic efforts of our nursing fraternity not only to cope with the COVID pandemic, but also to keep up with the myriad tasks which fall to this underappreciated group of workers. At the same time though, the sacrifices that they bear in relation to COVID, worldwide and not just here at home, has perhaps given Nurses Day a greater prominence this year than in the past.

The day itself, instituted since 1965, is observed around the world to pay tribute to the significant contribution that nurses have made, and continue to make, to human society and the health and well-being of the world's peoples over the years. May 12 marks the birth date of the woman who is today considered "the founder of modern nursing". She left not only a legacy for others to follow but put a female stamp on the profession which endures to this day.

More and more, men have been joining the profession even though in some societies the old sexual division of labour continues to result in many men frowning at participation in such a profession. It makes the decision of those men who take up nursing as a career even more admirable.

Nurses are among what is today regarded as the category of "frontline workers". It is to them, first and foremost that the everyday care of the sick, the ailing and aged is entrusted. They are the bedside carers, the minders, the morale boosters who often make a difference in the recovery of the sick. When relatives of the hospitalised for instance have long gone to rest at home, it is the nurses who are charged with the overnight vigil and trying to keep patients safe until next day.

It is a task which calls for special skills and a particular disposition making the nurse an extraordinary human being. The job of a nurse is by far not an easy one and can at times be most unpleasant. They are exposed to all kinds of human sicknesses and diseases which place not only them, but their families as well at risk.

Their contribution, forbearance and patience are not always appreciated and all too often they are subject to abuse, verbal and otherwise by members of the public. Yet when the chips are down, it is on the same nurses that we must rely, whether at hospitals, clinics, nursing homes or in our own domestic settings.

Their conditions of work are not always what they ought to be, the necessities for ensuring the success of their efforts are not always forthcoming and unfortunately, they are the ones who experience the brunt of the complaints and abuse. It is a situation which can test most human beings and from time to time the responses may not be in keeping with the responsibilities of the noble profession.

But overall, nurses all around the world have served the world's population well. They continue to do so in the face of the COVID threat, literally being on the frontline. They deserve not only our commendation but also our support for better working conditions, and appreciation as they carry out their thankless tasks. It is the least we can do.

– SEARCHLIGHT newspaper, editorial May 15, 2020

Abuse of Female Domestic Workers Must Be Ended

I had originally planned to use this week's column to focus on some current political issues but as I remembered that this Friday, today November 25, is International Day for the Elimination of Violence against Women, I decided instead to turn attention to a major problem still facing thousands of our women: this is the abuse of domestic workers.

That is not to say that this is how we must regard this important annual occasion. Indeed, this year, not only will November 25 continue the fight against the physical and emotional abuse of women, in the home, at workplaces and in the society at large, but it will also mark the start of an international campaign over the next 16 days leading up to Human Rights Day on December 10. This campaign is aimed at focusing global attention more deeply on measures to eliminate such violence against women by calling citizens to take appropriate action to show how much they care about the issue and to demand that governments take firmer action to rid our societies of this scourge.

These are not just worthwhile but essential measures, for though very often we as citizens express abhorrence when we hear the news of extreme actions of violence against women, whether in the home or the society as a whole, many violent actions occur daily and pass under the radar. Sadly, in spite of all the demonstrations, rallies, resolutions and so on emanating from November 25 actions, too many people, all around the world, continue to take violence against women for granted as if it is natural, perhaps the "punishment" for the "original sin" as some contend. Shockingly, too many of our women now seem to accept this fatalistic view and it is shocking to hear of how many acts of violence against women, not just physical mind you, continue to be tolerated in our societies. It is all the more reason why we should, in one way or another, give our support for campaigns such as those around November 25 and urge our women and their organizations to step up their campaigns. Surely our local women's organizations can do much better.

Today, this column takes the opportunity to extend the campaign for the rights of women to another area much overlooked in our society and in the world at large – the abuse of the rights of domestic workers. The international organization, Human Rights Watch states, "Tens of millions of women and girls are employed as domestic workers in private households". In such a private domestic setting, they do all kinds of work – clean, cook, take care of children and the elderly and perform other tasks, and errands, deemed "essential" by their employers.

While generally, there are national regulations governing their terms and conditions of employment, the reality is that needing to work to help take care of their families and largely not organized in any recognized grouping, they are forced to "toe the line" and accept tasks and conditions of work outside the framework of the law. It is amazing that even women who are active in demanding rights for women in the society as a whole, do not respect such "full" rights for their domestic employees. These employees must do as they are told and subject themselves to the whims and fancies of their employers. Such are the pressures, especially on women who are single parent heads of households, that they are reluctant to complain officially for fear of losing their jobs. In small societies like ours, social status can mean a lot.

It is all well and good to point to legislation and domestic regulations, social reality is another thing. How often do we hear of the contribution of female domestic workers being extolled? Are their invaluable contributions in carrying out domestic work appreciated and rewarded? Are we aware how many of them also have to put up with domestic abuse and sometimes even sexual exploitation by male employers?

In the absence of an organized campaign to end these abuses, they will continue. These domestic workers and their families are often treated as "inferior" to their employers and their families as though economic status overrides basic human rights. Even our local trade unions have not paid sufficient attention, in some cases none at all, to the plight of domestic workers. Some end up working longer-than-prescribed hours; sometimes on holidays without requisite remuneration, and getting to and from work, to private out-of-the way addresses, can be a huge problem.

These are problems that these women cannot solve by themselves. I want to urge the labour movement to lead the way. Let us not approach it from the standpoint of this union or that union benefitting; but of accomplishing the task of organizing the sector. The Labour Department can and must play an important role in this, and the government, which boasts of its being a "government of labour", must treat this as a very special situation and give every support. We cannot have these women who take care of our children and parents enduring these unnecessary hardships. Other organizations such as those representing Christians, women and other civil society groups must lend a hand also.

Our female domestic workers need and deserve our wholehearted support.

– SEARCHLIGHT *newspaper, November 15,2022*

International Women's Day

IWD and Women

On this occasion of the celebration of IWD (March 8, 1978), we the women of YULIMO call for equal legal rights for women and for:

(1) Equal pay for equal work, regardless of sex.

(2) An end to discrimination in employment practices and in all other areas of life.

(3) The institution of a reasonable period of paid maternity leave for all working women and the setting up of state-run day-care centres for the care of children and working mothers.

(4) Equal opportunities and benefits for children born of unmarried women.

(5) Equality of women with men before the law in all areas.

(6) Compulsory education at primary school level and free secondary school education for our children.

(7) A national Adult Education programme aimed at the complete wiping out of illiteracy.

(8) Special state protection and benefits for the aged, pregnant women and children.

(9) A sound economic programme aimed at securing national and public control of our national resources and providing employment for all capable of working.

(10) Proper housing and medical programmes to put an end to the current disgraceful situation in these fields.

(11) A National Food Programme for the provision of basic foods at a cheap rate as well as educating the population about the nutritional value of certain types of foods.

(12) A campaign against prostitution and venereal diseases.

(13) An end to malnutrition and gastroenteritis and all other childhood diseases.

– FREEDOM, *March 10, 1978*

IWD and the Progressive Movement

The local progressive movement can take much of the credit for placing International Women's Day (IWD) on the local calendar.

It was on March 8, 1974, that a group of young brothers and sisters from YULIMO (Youlou United Liberation Movement), then only 11 months old and not officially launched, together with their counterparts from ARWEE of Diamond Village, and the Local Entertainers Association of Robert "Patches" Knights, organized the first-ever IWD activities in St. Vincent and the Grenadines.

A cultural rally and exhibition were held at the Peace Memorial Hall to mark the occasion. The cultural influence of Africa was strongly reflected in the dress, song, poetry and drumming of the participants.

From then on, except for minor lapses, IWD has been commemorated in one form or another with rallies not only in Kingstown but extending as far as Chateaubelair on the Leeward coast and Diamond Village and Georgetown on the Windward.

One particularly memorable rally was the one held in 1983 at the Campden Park Industrial site which focused specifically on the problems of working women. This was again breaking new ground.

Such rallies laid the foundation for broader national activities, beginning in 1984 with the formation of an International Women's Day Committee. The success of this was reflected in the holding of the first-ever IWD march. Marches followed by rallies have also been held in each of the last ten years.

Initiatives for Action

Besides marches and rallies, serious discussions, seminars and consultations have been held over the years for IWD at which issues facing women, and areas of action to solve problems have been identified, discussed and agreed upon.

Such was the 1977 discussion at the Charles Verbeke Centre near Victoria Park, the original site of the St Martin's School, out of which steps were taken to form a Consumers' League. Other notable panels were those at the Sion Lodge (Sion Hill) in 1978; a 1980 seminar at the UWI Extra-Mural Centre and a Convention at Layou in 1985.

Naturally, JUSTICE newspaper and its predecessor, FREEDOM, have played their part along with the VINCENTIAN newspaper.

Such is the rich, but not so long history of IWD locally.

– JUSTICE, *March 13,1987*

International Advances for Women, But SVG Still Lagging

International Women's Day this year was marked by two very positive developments where the advancement of women globally is concerned. The first of these came in a surprising quarter, Hollywood, long considered a bastion of male chauvinism, with women generally acknowledged more for their physical attributes than for the skills they undoubtedly possess on an equal scale with men. At the prestigious OSCARS, the annual ceremony where the outstanding performances and films of the Hollywood film year receive their accolades, the 2010 awards for both Best Film and Best Director went to a woman, Kathryn Bigelow. In a curious twist of fate, her HURT LOCKER, a low-budget film, edged out the box-office blockbuster and favourite AVATAR, while she got the Best Director award ahead of her ex-husband, James Cameron.

It was the first time in 82 years that a female Director had taken the award. Fittingly, it came right on the eve of International Women's Day, a just reward for all those years of largely unrewarded effort. Ms. Bigelow was only the fourth female film-maker to be even nominated for the Directors Oscar all these years, reflecting the gender imbalance in the film world. *The Celluloid Ceiling*, published by San Diego University in the USA, reports that of the top 250 major earning films in the USA in 2009, only 7% were directed by women, incidentally a fall by 2% from the previous year and the same percentage as in 1987. In addition to centuries-old male biases, the difficult nature of a director's job and the problems of reconciling it with family life are among the explanations for the low female presence.

The second bit of encouraging news for women all over the world came on International Women's Day itself. The Indian Upper House of Parliament, the Rajya Sabha, on March 8 voted in favour of a Bill to reserve one-third of the seats in the National Parliament, and all state Assemblies, for women. Currently, the percentage of women representation in the Indian Lower House of Parliament, the Lok Sabha, stands at a mere 10%, less than even in St. Vincent and the Grenadines. The Bill now addresses this, with much expectation of approval, given the support by all major parties for the measure. While there has been widespread support for the historic step, the occasion was marred by the protests of some Parliamentarians, seven of whom had to be ejected for disorderly behaviour. This protest ignores the fact that, 62 years after achieving National Independence, equality for women in that great country is still far from reality. Political representation at the highest levels in India lags behind that of its neighbours: Pakistan has 30% female representation in Parliament; Bangladesh 15% and even war-torn Afghanistan has a 27% count.

The affirmative action of the Indian Parliament will, if nowhere else, certainly meet with a warm reception from the 54th Session of the United Nations Commission on the Status of Women. That body has been reviewing women's progress in precisely that area. As it stands now, the Scandinavian countries lead the world with Sweden boasting a 47% female representation. Trinidad and Tobago and Barbados are leaders in the Caribbean, but interestingly, as far as considering the proportion of Ministers of Government of the female sex, the 2007 Government of Grenada was in the lead in the Caribbean with a 50% ratio.

This issue of female political representation was addressed in this column on October 7 last year, in the run-up to the referendum on the Constitution. Now with elections very much on the cards and the political temperature rising, it is again an issue which must be placed in the forefront. Our approach to the choice of a new Parliament cannot simply be one of a choice of party. Every Party seeking our approval must address important sectoral interests as they try to grapple with inbuilt prejudices and discriminatory practices. The status of women and their opportunities for achieving equity must be a priority. Are the contenders addressing these? Are our women sufficiently organised and conscious to demand that political parties address their interests? Women are the bedrock of the support of the political parties here, but once again it seems that their representation in Parliament will be minimal. The Opposition NDP has only been able to put forward one female candidate among the 15 named, and from all indications, the governing party will muster no more than three from 15. Hopefully, with the proposed increase to a 17-constituency Parliament, there will be at least two women from among those nominated to contest the two additional seats.

The irony of all this is that the proposed new Constitution, rejected by the electorate on November 25 last, had, partially, tried to address this imbalance in gender representation in our Parliament. Besides Secs. 11, 17 and 21 of the Guiding Principles of Chapter 2, there was a specific recommendation in Sec. 21 (3) :

"Political parties are obliged to aspire to not having less than 30% of the combined total number of persons whose names are included on the Party Lists...as women and not less than 30%...as men."

While to some of us this proposal could have gone further, we the people were not even so forward-thinking and out went even that mild progression in our NO vote in the referendum. Now we are stuck with the consequences and our women, for all their campaigning and fund-raising, will again have limited representation in the new Parliament. This year's IWD again underlined the fundamental weakness of the women's movement here. Just one week before, hundreds of women had lined up on opposite sides of the political battle lines outside Parliament, in support of their respective parties, but come International Women's Day, neither of their parties could help them mobilise to promote their own specific interests as women. Is this all our political women are willing to settle for? What of the much-vaunted educated and professional women? Women's political representation is not the be-all-and-end-all, but it is a necessary step in the right direction. Our women must be prepared to take leadership on this score.

– SEARCHLIGHT *newspaper, March 12, 2010*

Women's Day Must Bring Us Together

I was really happy to hear of the honouring of three female farmers: Nioka Abbott-Balcombe of Langley Park; Cordelia Scott of Georgetown and Norgie Tucker of Chateaubelair, as part of this year's International Women's Day (IWD) activities.

These were accolades well-deserved, both on account of their own productive contribution in the field, but more so, the tremendous contribution they made, and continue to make, socially. They have demonstrated that women can organize, can inspire, not just other women, but their men folk as well. In addition to this, they have done so beyond the agricultural field and have made tremendous contributions to rural community socio-economic development.

I got to know all three and to work, at some time or other, with them, during my more than two decades with WINFA, and I am comforted that WINFA, in spite of the challenges facing it and the sector, not only upholds the International Women's Day tradition, but does not forget the humble nation-builders. There are many more like them whom we must extol; put aside the negatives arising from our own pettiness, and hold up as examples for generations following.

The activity, a collaborative one between the Ministry of Agriculture, IICA and WINFA, was one of a number of different types of activities held to mark IWD. They included one organized by the Gender Affairs Department, focusing on female students and another, by the National Council of Women (NCW), which concentrated on women and media skills. Hats off to both and to the other less-reported but equally important IWD initiatives!

However, I am still not satisfied with the level of preparation and celebration of such a signal occasion in the national and international calendars. I admit to being particularly attached hereto, given my own involvement in social and political organizations over the years for whom, Women's Day, Workers' Day, Emancipation Day, African Liberation Day, National Heroes Day and Independence Day, were, each in their own right, accorded prominence. Perhaps now we can see the difference between the pioneering organizations and the narrow political organizations of today.

I say so because women play fundamental roles in the building and sustenance of our political parties. We are just out of an election, and during this period and the petty storms after, women have been in the forefront of the battles, on one side or the other. Yet when occasions like IWD come around, where is the comparable level of support for the cause of women, across-the-board, NDP or ULP? Where are the mobilization efforts? If we are talking reconciliation, is not the cause of women, irrespective of political affiliation, deserving of the unreserved support of both political parties in urging women to unite for a common cause, the cause of ALL WOMEN on IWD?

But maybe I am day-dreaming, for the political will to respond to numerous calls by international bodies such as the United Nations and Organization of American States (OAS), among others, to make resolute efforts to ensure greater female representation in Parliament, Cabinet, and decision-making, seems not to exist, in one camp or the other. Yes, there are challenges, but so too in many other spheres of life; why are we so timid on this one? And, why do our women, so vocal and active in campaigning, accept the lame excuses?

One standard answer we get when these issues are raised is that women are the biggest beneficiaries of education, which has propelled them to many executive positions, especially in the public service. That is undoubtedly true, but it masks a number of other realities. Where is the strong female presence beyond that? How come, almost 40 years after Independence, the post of Minister of Gender Affairs, (it used to be Women's Affairs) has been held for the majority of time by men? Given the still unresolved issues confronting women, when are we, all of us, ULP, NDP or otherwise, going to repose confidence in our women to take that responsibility fully?

As for the "education" talk, regarding women, it will be useful to refer to a study by the International Labour Organization (ILO) just released to mark IWD 2016, which notes that while there has been "significant progress" by women in education during the last two decades, these have not been translated into improvements at the work-place. The study points out that despite an almost equal spread between male and female in the global population, more men (two billion) were employed last year than women (1.3 billion) and consequently more women were unemployed, particularly young women. This has grave social consequences.

Then there is discrimination including in the pay packet. Women work longer hours than men, the study concludes, do more unpaid household work and there is a gender gap between the pay of female and male workers of about 23 per cent, which, it is estimated, will take 70 years to eradicate. Finally, because women are less employed, they have less access to retirement and pension benefits, so that in our world today over 200 million women are living without a regular income from old age or survivors' pensions.

Does this not tell us why IWD is relevant to all women and the society as a whole? The challenges facing women have no party affiliation; they need broad cross-party action and unity to address them. IWD provides a focal point. Let us use it effectively.

– SEARCHLIGHT *newspaper, March 11, 2016.*

IWD – Rooting Out Violence Against Our Women

Another International Women's Day (IWD) has come around and, once more, we cannot escape from having the issue of violence against women as one of the primary focus matters. In addition to the weekly reports and court cases, this year the shocking slaughter of a Cuban-trained nurse, Sis. Arianna Duharte Taylor Israel, on a school compound in full view of students, has brought this burning issue forcefully to the forefront. Her husband has been charged with the murder.

I can only hope that, and indeed urge, the organisers of the various IWD activities to find some time during their deliberations to remember and pay tribute to this wonderful daughter of Cuba.

From reports of all those who came into contact with her, especially as she carried out her nursing duties, Arianna was exceptional in her devotion to her profession, in the warmth and care she displayed. I have heard this even from persons politically misguided in their opposition to Cuba and Cuban personnel here, but who were touched by the quality of her service to them. It is a reminder of the debt we owe to Cuba and its dedicated internationalists; a debt that many of us do not acknowledge or for which we do not sufficiently demonstrate our gratitude. Arianna was a shining example of this internationalism manifested in the improvement of our health services and our international airport.

Her murder has not only shocked the society, but once more highlighted the vulnerability of our women. It has re-ignited calls for an all-out campaign to rid our society of this scourge and to treat our women with the respect that they deserve.

We have marked previous IWD occasions and the International Day for the Elimination of Violence Against Women (Nov. 25) with marches and rallies demanding an end be put to this evil.

Unfortunately, these stirring appeals, though necessary, are not enough to eliminate this blight on our society. For one, many of the perpetrators and potential perpetrators of such violence are either not listening or are entirely unaware of the extent to which they are prone to such dastardly deeds. Violence against and abuse of women is deeply rooted in our society, originating from its character as being male dominated, a condition which women are supposed to accept.

There are even some who attempt to use Biblical quotations to support this ridiculous falsehood!

Worse, it is also a legacy of a slave society when the master could use, abuse and cast aside slave women at will. There are still remnants of that among our men today and violence is used as an instrument to enforce male dominance. It is reflected in the way that we treat our women. In the 21st century there are still young men, macho spirit and all, who refer to women as "the thing", a manifestation of the misguided thinking behind this expression. Logically therefore, it is right to use violence to defend one's "thing", one's "property".

Tackling this deep-rooted malignancy needs, in addition to our prayers, appeals and marches, a concerted effort throughout all levels of the society.

We need to understand the complexity of the problem; the frailty of men who think that their "natural right" to dominance is being threatened; to unhook it from outdated and misguided religious teachings, and to recognize that we all deserve equal treatment, irrespective of gender, race, class, religious or political perspectives.

We continue to bring up our children accepting this supposed "right" of the male to dominate but expect to instill a different outlook when they become adults. We accept the dominance of the powerful over the powerless and the right of might in international affairs. War is still seen as a tool for enforcing one's will, not as a ruthless destroyer of human life and the environment.

It is easy then to accept violence against women, we become outraged when we believe that it is "overdone", not by the very concept itself.

These are some of the issues we have to begin to reflect on as we celebrate IWD. Women suffered violently the world over for demanding their rights and those rights are still being trampled upon, including in the home. It is a fight from which we must not shirk and must take up in the home, in our schools, churches, and institutions, and insist that the institutions of law and order, the police and courts respect as well.

Have a reflective IWD!

– SEARCHLIGHT *newspaper, March 6, 2020*

IWD 2022 – Much to Celebrate

Next Tuesday, March 8, women all around the world will be celebrating another International Women's Day, a day specifically to focus on the status of women, their needs and progress especially in such fundamental matters as equality and advancement where power relations are concerned.

This year the theme chosen reflects not only the particular interests of women but those of humanity as a whole. It speaks of, "Gender equality today for a sustainable tomorrow". In keeping with this theme is the explanation of "recognizing the contributions" of those who are leading the charge on climate change adaptation, mitigation and the response to build a sustainable future for all".

Interestingly, women are being encouraged to wear PURPLE on the day. It will be interesting to note to what extent this call will be heeded for even without any official prompting, women adopted RED as their colour of choice to mark the fictional "Valentine's Day".

IWD has particular significance for St Vincent and the Grenadines, for our women have been foremost in promoting its observation. Three years before the United Nations itself officially recognized the date of observation, in 1977, in SVG there was a public celebration of the event, at the Peace Memorial Hall in 1974, organized by the non-governmental organizations. Since then, it has largely been that sector which has kept the IWD flag flying with varying levels of commitment and support on the part of successive governments.

Its seeming decline in importance in recent years has much to do with the diminishing importance of the non-governmental sector and what is left of the organized women's movement in particular.

From year to year there have been some activities to mark the occasion but these have largely been ad hoc and focused on particular sectors rather than on the women's movement as a whole.

Yet this cannot dispute the fact that there has been noted progress in relation to the participation of women in national development and the recognition of the same. This is especially so in relation to education where more and more women are in the forefront. Indeed, women today play critical roles in relation to the administrative machinery of state and in social life as a whole.

While their participation at a decision-making level in parliament and the private sector as a whole leaves much room for improvement, the examples of persons like Ms. Shafia London, appointed the Barbados Country Manager for the world's largest brewery, can serve as an inspiration in that regard. Ms. London became, just two years ago, the first Vincentian, man or woman, to become Country Manager of our own SVG Brewery.

Overall though, the achievements of women have been largely individual rather than collective. Could it be because those achievements remain at that singular level and are not reflected in the building of a united Women's Movement to address the long-outstanding issues continuing to plague our women?

From time to time, we witness campaigns on such burning issues as violence against women, but there is not enough connection with the myriad other issues which affect our women. The emphasis on the issues relating to climate change and sustainable development provide a unifying basis for addressing women's issues in particular and those of society as a whole.

Will our women take up this challenge in a collective effort?

– SEARCHLIGHT *newspaper, March 10, 2022*

IWD 2021 – Women, Let's Choose to Challenge Ourselves

When the women of St. Vincent and the Grenadines (SVG) join our sisters all over the world next Monday to celebrate International Women's Day (IWD), we will do so in the knowledge that there is much that we have to celebrate, much of which to be proud. This year, the United Nations has chosen as the theme for the occasion, "Women in Leadership: Achieving an equal future in a Covid–19 world". It is a most fitting theme indeed, given the effects of the global pandemic on women, children and families as pointed out in our Midweek editorial of March 2.

Complementing this is the campaign theme for this year's activities, #ChooseToChallenge. It has been chosen so that all, not just women, can choose to challenge and call out gender bias and inequity and in this way collectively help to create an inclusive world.

Women in SVG have been making headway where leadership positions are concerned. Our country has a female Head of State, one of only 20 countries worldwide to have a woman as either Head of State or Government. Our Parliament is presided over by a woman with another as her deputy to boot, and female Senators sit on both sides of the House. There is an impressive list of female leaders in the legal and medical professions, in managerial positions in the private sector as well as a bevy of female entrepreneurs, along with female dominance in the public service and prominence at the leadership level in a host of social organisations. We are well placed in this regard and on Monday our women are entitled to "Take a Bow".

Yet, in spite of these meritorious positions, women's influence does not seem to be reflected adequately in the impact on public policy, especially on issues pertaining to women, children and the family. Our considerable social and political weight seems not to be brought to bear in influencing public policy and its effect on women.

Take the continuing scourges of violence against women, sexual exploitation and harassment and the problems encountered on an ongoing basis by female domestic workers, and women in the hospitality industry. Our women have reached too far in social, economic and political life to be confined to annual marches calling for an end to violence against women. We possess the collective capacity to do something about it. So, as we applaud the achievements and celebrate the advances, some collective soul-searching is needed. Why is there no vibrant national umbrella women's organisation, uniting all the diverse strands and bringing the collective experience and wisdom of women to bear on the problems facing us? Are we satisfied with the current state of activity or influence of the national Council of Women or the impact of the Department of Gender Affairs?

We thank those women who are already doing their best in our interests, but what of other, more influential women? Are we too busy with our own advances to make the sacrifices necessary to organize collective action? The lack of unity and coordination at such an essential level is severely limiting the scope of women's influence. Women cannot content themselves to be mere images of men in leadership positions. We have had women as Ministers of government from as far back as the sixties but their impact on public policy in favour of women has been rather limited.

We cannot afford to let such a rich array of talent go to waste. Collective effort is needed to coordinate all the noble initiative at the personal and individual organisational levels. Choose to challenge ourselves, dear women of SVG. #ChooseToChallenge

– SEARCHLIGHT *newspaper, editorial, March 5, 2023*

Making Gender Equality a Reality

Special greetings to all my sisters – the women of St. Vincent and the Grenadines and the world over on the occasion of the celebration of International Women's Day, March 8th. In these days when the buzz word is all about GENDER, it is not so fashionable to be talking of Women's Day. Who knows? Some crank may soon come up with the idea of an International Day for the Focus on Gender Relations, and depending on who puts it forward, it may even gain support. I want though, to keep the focus on WOMEN.

It is now over 30 years since we here in St. Vincent and the Grenadines first organized activities to mark IWD. Like most other positive developments, it was the progressive movement which first introduced and celebrated IWD here. In 1974, the still fledgling organizations like BLAC, OBCA, ARWEE and LEA (Local Entertainers Association), not only combined to commemorate African Liberation Day, in May, but fully two months before that, they pioneered the organization of the first-ever IWD activities to be held in SVG. Those activities were held at the Peace Memorial Hall on March 8th, 1974 and were a combined effort of young women and men working together for a common purpose. Talk about gender relations?

We have come a long way since. The United Nations had by then placed the struggle for women's rights, respect and equality on an official footing and many governments, whether half heartedly, or (as we would say it colloquially) in "follow-fashion", also adopted solemn proclamations on the rights of women. Legal and practical steps were taken, with varying degrees of committedness and success, to raise the standard of living and being of women. Following on this we had "Women's Desk," " Ministries of Women Affairs' ' and a plethora of committees and organizations all aimed at ensuring the upliftment of our women folk.

Three decades on, there are many tangible signs of progress. In some societies like ours, women today dominate the more humane professions such as teaching and nursing. They are prominent in the public service and the legal profession. They make important contributions to the service sector and gradually are emerging in fields once considered the sole preserve of men. The socio-political emphasis on education and health has contributed immeasurably to those positive developments.

Yet we are still far from the lofty goals and objectives set. Policy making, at the political level and in critical areas of national policy, is still overwhelmingly driven by men, in stark contrast either to the proportion of women in our society or their real contribution to national development. In many critical social areas, we seem to have regressed where respect for women by men, and by women themselves are concerned. Not only is there widespread crimes of violence against women–rape and sexual assault, wife and spouse-beating, incest and molestation - but in spite of our loud pronouncements we seem to accept these as "realities of life".

Where the livelihood of women is concerned, important social contributors such as domestics, women in the hospitality industry and those involved in public sanitation, vendors and women farmers are all still regarded as having lesser social status. Our failure to be able to dis-aggregate valuable statistics on the basis of gender leaves us with only a partial analysis of our problems and a consequent falling short in prescriptive remedies. Thus we can take the relatively high levels of women involved in teaching, the public service or agriculture as positive signs of women's advancement. But it may well be that they are there in numbers, sometimes by virtue of being entrapped by conjugal or familial situations or because men, for one reason or another, have more opportunities for lateral or vertical mobility. That is certainly true of many female-headed households, some families are completely abandoned by the men.

For all of these reasons, and given our historical developments, the issues of women's equality and equity in gender relations need to be addressed in a far more comprehensive manner than we have managed so far. A lot of the responsibility for this must be borne by our women themselves. If our women only pay one-tenth of the attention to building a vigorous national women's movement as they pay to the fortunes of the two political parties, ULP and NDP, then not only they, but the entire society would be much better off for it. If the partisanship in politics can instead be directed positively towards remedying the discrimination and exploitation of women, then we would truly be taking a giant step forward towards making the goal of the United Nations' Millennium Development Goals, a reality, namely.

PROMOTE GENDER EQUALITY AND EMPOWER WOMEN

– SEARCHLIGHT *newspaper, March 7, 2008*

General

Just A Kiss? / Oh Africa!

This week, the column focuses on two current international situations which, though far away from our shores, have implications for all of us. I begin with the unfortunate situation which has developed in Spain following that country's victory in the 2023 Women's World Cup of football.

JUST A KISS?

That situation was the reprehensible action of the President of the Spanish Football Federation in grabbing the head of one of the Spanish players, Jenni Hermoso, and planting a full-blooded kiss on her mouth, apparently as a means of congratulation. A weird interpretation, I must say. Immediately there was negative worldwide reaction, understandably so. It is one thing to kiss a person on the cheek as is accepted in many countries, but all and sundry could see the action on television, and it must stretch the imagination to call this a congratulatory smack.

But that was only the first ripple of the storm, for following the global criticism, there was a senseless reaction by both the offending official, Luis Robiales, and the Spanish Federation. They rubbished the criticism and gave support to Robiales's claim that the kiss was "consensual", and in fact put pressure on the senorita to say words to that effect. Now why would she agree to a public consensual kiss in front of the view of the world? And why would the President want to do such a thing?

Buoyed by this apparent show of support, Robiales aggressively addressed his membership in the face of calls for his resignation, defiantly refusing to do so and even being applauded by some members of his Federation. But that is when things began to go awry. The offended player made it plain that it was not a "consensual kiss" and that she was sexually assaulted as seemed obvious from the live coverage.

In addition, she received the backing of not only the Spanish team but a wider cross-section of leading players who declared that they would not play for Spain if no action was taken. The Spanish World Cup coaches, bar one, the Head Coach, who had been backed by Robiales in a pre-World Cup dispute, also resigned. Much more was to follow.

The sexual assault and dismissal of it as "just a kiss" came in the wake of widespread allegations of racism in Spanish football. Now racism and sexism are social bedfellows, both increasingly unacceptable in the modern world, including sport. It came to the attention of Spain, its government and football authorities, that their joint bid with Portugal and Morocco to stage the 2030 FIFA World Cup was in jeopardy if Spanish football was tainted with these twin stains.

So, there came a sudden about-turn with the Spanish authorities calling for Robiales's resignation and even prosecution. Spanish interests were now in jeopardy and Robiales and his "kiss' were to be jettisoned.

But the whole matter is bigger than all of this. It relates to the age-old apparent privilege of people in positions of power to abuse women and get away with it. "What happen ? Why you getting on so? Is only a kiss!", some would say; or a mere "touch on the breast", or buttock. It is an assault on the rights of women and must be ended. Women of SVG are physically far from the scene but they know the scenario. Speak out now so that all those here who contemplate or practice such behaviour must be brought to heel.

"Just a kiss", they say. Tell them where to kiss...

OH AFRICA!

The Caribbean, with countries like St Vincent and the Grenadines and Barbados leading the charge, is quite correctly pursuing its destiny in forging closer relations with Africa. Trade and economic relations, cultural cooperation and global coordination on matters like climate change and reparations are the main issues on the agenda.

But what must be worrying to Caribbean countries, certainly their people if not all their leaders, is the constant instability on the continent, the propensity of leaders towards undemocratic rule, lasting decades in some instances, which themselves tend to create the conditions for military intervention in the forms of coups. Too often though, these coups, often welcomed by people anxious to be rid of leaders displaying undemocratic tendencies, veer away from their populist origins and sometimes require further military intervention. Thus, the cycle continues.

The latest of these, just weeks after a coup in Niger, came on Wednesday this week in the oil and mineral-rich country of Gabon in central Africa. There, the people have been plagued by a parasitic family, the Bongo family, living "high off the hog" and in conjunction with foreign corporations and the military protection of France, the biggest parasite in African flesh, bleeding precious resources while leaving the people to wallow in poverty.

I shall develop this theme in later columns but suffice it to say, that we cannot be talking "oneness" with Africa, unless we also show interest in democracy there, support resistance to the continued rape of African resources and the support by foreign countries for undemocratic regimes which suppress the African people. We have a stake in that also.

– SEARCHLIGHT newspaper, September 1, 2023

Thank You, Mama.

How nice it would be if, come Sunday morning, May 14, Vincentians wake up to the strains of Becket's epic, "Thank You, Mama", in honour of Mothers' Day! Though the date differs for different countries in the world, the idea of paying homage to our mothers globally does not change and each country has its own traditions. The importance of the occasion cannot be over emphasized.

Mothers' Day is one of two global occasions specifically set aside to remember and pay respect to the contributions of women in the development of human society, the other being International Women's Day.

Not all women are mothers, so while International Women's Day has a naturally wider focus and tends to focus on women's rights and achievements, Mothers' Day has tended to have a narrower focus, on the contributions of mothers, especially in the home and family.

Like everything else in society, the nature of its celebration changes with time. There were times when its importance seemed to be growing here in St Vincent and the Grenadines with a number of social activities organized for the occasion; but there were other times, depending on broader societal developments, when it has been less prominent. Yet Becket's enduring thanks remain.

He expresses profuse thanks to our mothers "for all the things you do for me". We thus remember the arduous, and often thankless tasks of child rearing, not just by more mature and equipped women in families, but often foisted upon young ones quite unprepared for such a critically important task. However, there are sometimes what is called the seamier side of it, the things that mothers are sometimes forced to do to support their children and their upbringing, often painful secrets divulged only to very close companions.

Some of these, forced on the most vulnerable, remain like an eternal shame and blot on their lives. It rubs salt into wounds later, when some of those who have benefited from the suffering imposed on their very mothers seem not to appreciate or reciprocate the sacrifices involved.

As we mark this occasion, given the difficult economic and social conditions, it is important that we pay special attention in our society to the development of young mothers, teenage and pre-teen mothers among them. There has been some mention made in recent years about the role of young fathers in helping to rear our children.

For Mothers' Day 2023, let us spare some thoughts for such young mothers. Each time we get the reports of the senseless murder of young men, just remember that many of these are themselves fathers, leaving young women, often ill-equipped to cope with responsibilities of dual parenting.

There has to be a way for our society, our institutions of state, church and community to help them to develop and handle such formidable responsibilities.

Our very future as a society depends on it.

– SEARCHLIGHT *newspaper, May 12, 2023*

About the Author

Renwick Ellsworth Adrian Rose, also known as "Kamara", is a distinguished political and social activist from St. Vincent and the Grenadines. Born to Reynold Rose, a tailor, and his wife Germaine, an early childhood educator, Rose has spent more than 50 years championing the causes of the poor and marginalized in the Caribbean.

In the early 1970s, Rose challenged the political status quo by becoming a foundation member of the Black Liberation Action Committee (BLAC) and later the Youlou United Liberation Movement (YULIMO), advocating for genuine independence and socialism. In 1979, YULIMO merged with other groups to form the United People's Movement (UPM), with Rose as one of its leaders. He worked to raise political awareness among Vincentians and fostered regional and international networks to amplify the voices of the masses.

Between 1974 and 1989, as a journalist, Rose managed and edited several newspapers, including FREEDOM, JUSTICE, and JUSTSPORTS. He was a weekly columnist in the NEWS newspaper from 1989 to 1994 and has been a weekly columnist in the SEARCHLIGHT newspaper since 1995. He has also, over the years, made many written contributions to the VINCENTIAN newspaper. Rose's journalism plays a crucial role in informing and mobilizing the public on important civic, social and political issues.

He joined the Windward Islands Farmers Association (WINFA) in 1989 as a programme officer, later becoming its coordinator until his retirement in 2010. He facilitated farmer exchanges and liaised with francophone members, enhancing regional agricultural cooperation.

Rose remains an advocate for civil society participation in governance. He was one of the founders of the St. Vincent and the Grenadines Civil Society Forum and later chaired the National Economic Social Development Council (NESDEC), promoting dialogue between government, private sector, and civil society. Rose was one of the leading members of the 2009 Constitutional Reform Committee and is considered one of the first feminists in St. Vincent and the Grenadines.

Regionally, he promotes civil society cooperation and at the time of his retirement was the chairman of the regional civil society movement, the Caribbean Policy Development Centre (CPDC).

Rose has received numerous awards for his contributions to politics, sports, media, and nation-building. His unwavering commitment to equal rights, justice, and sustainable livelihoods continues to inspire and drive strategic change across the Caribbean.

www.ingramcontent.com/pod-product-compliance
Lightning Source LLC
Chambersburg PA
CBHW060529030426
42337CB00021B/4189